This book is for you

you

_____

From me

me

_____

On this day

day

_____

Because

because

_____

Dare to
BE

70 Questions
That Lead to
Life's Most
Important
Answers

by John Mason

Bridge-Logos

Gainesville, Florida 32614

Bridge-Logos

Gainesville, FL 32614 USA

Dare to BE
by John Mason

Copyright ©2006 by Bridge-Logos

Printed in the United States of America.

Library of Congress Catalog Card Number: 2006902170
International Standard Book Number 0-88270-153-3

Scripture quotations are from the *King James Version* of the Bible unless otherwise noted.

G163.316.N.m604.35250

Dedication

It's an honor to dedicate this book to my awesome family.

Who always leaves me better than she found me?

 My wife, Linda.

Who is a friend you can always depend on?

 My daughter, Michelle.

Who makes me laugh everyday?

 My son, Greg.

Who is full of witty ideas and inventions?

 My son, Michael.

Who is always ready to beat me one-on-one?

 My son, David.

Acknowledgments

Special thanks to my pastor and friend, Ed Gungor. He first posed the question, "What if it's true?" to me. That question and his ministry are helping me discover the joy of authentic Christian life.

Thanks to David Blunt. His sincere questions have challenged and inspired me since the beginning of my ministry.

Thank you to the staff of Bridge-Logos and my friend Guy Morrell. Their encouragement, enthusiasm, and expertise in publishing this book have been demonstrated from beginning to end.

Introduction

You've heard the old expression, "Look before you leap". Well, here's another bit of advice just as valuable. "Ask before you leap."

As you enter any new dimension in your life, there are questions you can ask that will lead you to answers you must have. There is one thing I know for certain: good questions lead to good answers.

This book, *Dare to Be*, gives you seventy indispensable questions for a lifetime of answers. It is the kind of book I wish I could have read when I was in my teens or twenties.

Read this book when you're alone, dreaming of what God has for you; share this book with others who are stuck or trying to work their way out of a mess; or discuss this book with your mentor, Mom or Dad.

I know God has answers for all of life's questions. He can reveal those to you when you ask the right questions.

Do you leave people better than you found them?

The People Investment

One of the most exciting decisions you can make is to be on the lookout for opportunities to invest in others. For me, this has been one of the most powerful principles of momentum I've implemented in my life.

About ten years ago, I remember driving to Tulsa, Oklahoma, from St. Louis, Missouri with my family. I was listening to a Zig Ziglar tape and on this tape he said, "You'll always have everything you want in life, if you'll help enough other people get what they want." When I heard this statement, literally, something went off inside of me, and I said out loud, "I'm going to do it." That decision to look for ways to help others, to invest in them, changed my life.

"There are three keys to more abundant living: caring about others, daring for others and sharing with others" (William Ward). Assign yourself the purpose of making others happy and successful. People have a way of becoming what you encourage them to be.

There are two types of people in the world: those who come into a room and say, "Here I am!" and those who come in and say, "Ah, there you are!" Do this: "If you cannot win, make the one ahead of you break the record" (Jan McKeithen). Invest in others. It pays great dividends.

Is the only time you do any deep praying when you find yourself in a hole?

Troubleshooting

If God is your father, please call home. Corrie ten Boom said, "The devil smiles when we make plans. He laughs when we get too busy. But he trembles when we pray."

"Don't worry about anything; instead, pray about everything; tell God your needs and don't forget to thank him for his answers. If you do this you will experience God's peace, which is far more wonderful than the human mind can understand" (Philippians 4:6-7, TLB). When you feel swept off your feet, it's time to go back on your knees.

"Time spent in communion with God is never lost," says Gordon Lindsay. The highest purpose of faith or prayer is not to change your circumstances, but to change you. Pray to do the will of God in every situation; nothing else is worth praying for.

James Hudson Taylor put it this way: "Do not have your concert and tune your instruments afterwards. Begin the day with God." Martin Luther once said, "I have so much to do today that I shall spend the first three hours in prayer."

Prayer may not change all things for you, but it sure changes you for all things. He's waiting to hear from you.

Has failure gone to your head?

Renew the Blues

What is the difference between champions and the average person? Tom Hopkins says, "The single most important difference between champion achievers and average people is their ability to handle rejection and failure." You can't travel the road to success without a puncture or two.

Mistakes are often the best teachers. The book of Ecclesiastes advises, "In the day of prosperity be joyful, but in the day of adversity consider."

Oswald Avery advises, "Whenever you fall, pick something up." The man who invented the eraser had the human race pretty well figured out. David McNally mused, "The mistake-riddled life is much richer, more interesting, and more stimulating than the life that has never risked or taken a stand on anything."

Known for his successes, not his failures, Thomas Edison reflected, "People are not remembered by how few times they failed, but by how often they succeed."

Louis Boone said, "Don't fear failure so much that you refuse to try new things. The saddest summary of life contains three descriptions, could have, might have, and should have." Robert Schuller wrote, "Look at what you have left, never look at what you have lost."

Are you a person who says, "My decision is maybe— and that's final"?

Fencing

Is this you? Have you ever noticed that some of the most miserable people in the world are those who can never make a decision? Being decisive is an absolute key to a successful life. Every accomplishment, great or small, starts with a decision. Nothing great was ever done without a decision.

If you commit yourself to being indecisive, what kind of life will you live? James Hightower says, "There's nothing in the middle of the road but yellow stripes and dead armadillos." The truth is that the most dangerous place to be is in the middle of the road.

Do you lack opportunities? Make some decisions. The moment you definitely decide, all sorts of things happen to help you that never would have otherwise occurred. There is no question that you create opportunities by being decisive.

The book of James says, "A double-minded man is unstable in all his ways." Too many people go through life not knowing what they want, but feeling sure they don't have it. Remain indecisive and you will never grow. To move from where you are, you must decide where you would rather be.

Would the child you were be proud of the adult you are?

Walk Tall

Character is the real foundation of all worthwhile success. A good question to ask yourself is, "What kind of advice do I give others that I need to follow myself?" Living a double life will get you nowhere twice as fast. "Thoughts lead on to purposes; purposes go forth in action; actions form habits; habits decide character; and character fixes our destiny," said Tryon Edwards. Proverbs asserts, "A good name is rather to be chosen than great riches."

Would your reputation recognize your character if they met in the dark? Desire what Psalms declared, "Create in me a pure heart, Oh Lord, and renew in me a right spirit." To change your character, you must begin at the control center—the heart.

Consider what Woodrow Wilson said: "If you think about what you ought to do for people, your character will take care of itself." The world's best sermon is preached by the traffic sign: Keep Right.

In what areas do you claim faith, but your actions say unbelief?

Deliver the Goods

None of the secrets of success will work unless **you** do. The Bible, a book of faith, talks about work over 500 times. Often, the simple answer to your problem is: *go to work*.

"Be doers of the word not hearers only, deceiving yourselves" (James 1:22).

When you hear and don't do, you allow deception and inaccuracy to come into your life. That's why you know people who read good books, go to church, listen to tapes and are still a mess. They don't put into practice what they have learned. A famous old saying says it best: "Laziness travels so slowly, poverty soon overtakes it."

The world is divided into people who do things and people who talk about doing things. Belong to the first group—there is far less competition.

There is a man in the world who never gets turned
   down, wherever he chances to stray;
He gets the glad hand in the populous town, or out
   where the farmers make hay;
He is greeted with pleasure on deserts of sand, and
   deep in the isles of the woods;
Wherever he goes there is a welcoming hand, he's the
   man who delivers the goods. (Walt Whitman)

Are you having fun yet?

Sunny Smiles

There is a facelift you can perform on yourself that is guaranteed to improve your appearance. It's called a smile. Laughter is like changing a baby's diaper—it solves a problem and makes things more acceptable for awhile.

I believe that every time you smile, and even much more so when you laugh, you add something to your life. A smile is a curve that helps us see things straight. Janet Layne said, "Of all the things you wear, your expression is the most important." Proverbs says, "A merry heart doeth good like a medicine." A good laugh is the best medicine, whether you are sick or not.

The wheels of progress are not turned by cranks. Tom Walsh says, "Every minute your mouth is turned down you lose 60 seconds of happiness." Paul Bourge wrote, "Unhappiness indicates wrong thinking, just as ill health indicates a bad regime." It's impossible to smile on the outside without feeling better on the inside. If you can laugh at it, you can live with it. Smile, it adds to your face value.

It was only a sunny smile,
But it scattered the night.
Thus little it cost in giving,
It made the day worth living.

(Anonymous)

Does God seem far away? If so, guess who moved.

The God Habit

Oswald Chambers advises us: "Get into the habit of dealing with God about everything. Unless in the first waking moment of the day you learn to fling the door wide back and let God in, you will work on a wrong level all day; but swing the door wide open and pray to your Father in secret, and every public thing will be stamped with the presence of God." When God is all you have, then He is all you need.

"Draw near to God, and He will draw near to you" (James 4:8). The Bible also says that, "God inhabits the praises of his people." Good news! God is never more than a prayer or a praise away.

Tommy Barnett reflected, "The deeper I dig, the deeper He digs." To increase value, get to know God. Our prayer to God should be: "I want to be in your will, not in your way."

Our heartfelt cry to God can be the same as Isaiah's cry: "Here I am, send me" (Isaiah 6:8).

Consider the words of W. H. Atken when he said, "Lord take my lips and speak through them; take my mind and think through it; take my heart and set it on fire." We must not only give what we have, we must also give all of what we are to God.

Do you look at the horizon and see an opportunity, or do you look into the distance and fear a problem?

Fear Fighter

Fear is a poor chisel to carve out your tomorrows. If you are looking at your future from a position of fear, I want to let you know that view is inaccurate and distorted. It's never safe to look into the future with the eyes of fear. The worst liars in the world are your own fears. One of the great discoveries you can make is to find that you can do what you were afraid you couldn't do.

William Ward showed the difference between faith and worry: "Worry is faith in the negative, trust in the unpleasant, assurance of disaster and belief in defeat. Worry is a magnet that attracts negative conditions. Faith is a more powerful force that creates positive circumstances ... Worry is wasting today's time to clutter up tomorrow's opportunities with yesterday's troubles."

Dale Carnegie wrote, "An old man was asked what had robbed him of joy in his life. His reply was, 'Things that never happened.'" Fear wants you to run from things that aren't after you. Here's what I do. I follow this famous advice: "At night, I give all my worries and fears to God. He's going to be up all night anyway."

1 Peter 5:7 puts it this way: "Let Him have all your worries and cares, for He is always thinking about you and watching everything that concerns you."

Do you go where opportunity is, or where opportunity is going?

Big Game

Go farther than you can see. Don't just look at the present. Think unthinkable thoughts, see where no one is looking and take action before it's obvious. Wayne Gretsky is, arguably, the greatest hockey player in history. Asked about his secret for continuing to lead the national hockey league in goals year after year, Gretsky replied, "I skate to where the puck is going to be, not where it has been."

Isak Dineson said, "God made the world round so that we would never be able to see too far down the road." Significant achievements have never been obtained by taking small risks on unimportant issues. "If you're hunting rabbits in tiger country, you must keep your eye peeled for tigers, but when you are hunting tigers you can ignore the rabbits" (Henry Stern). Don't be distracted by the rabbits. Set your sights on "big game."

You have reached stagnation when all you ever exercise is caution. Too many people expect little, ask for little, receive little and are content with little. Having a dream is not trying to believe something regardless of the evidence; dreaming is daring to do something regardless of the consequences. Let your faith run ahead of your mind.

When it comes to giving, are you a person who will stop at nothing?

Go with the Flow

The secret to living is giving. One way to judge a person is by what they say. A better way is by what they do. The best way is by what they give. Charles Spurgeon said, "Feel for others—in your wallet." An Indian proverb says, "Good people, like clouds, receive only to give away." Whatever good happens in your life is not so you can keep it all to yourself. Part of it is intended to be given to others. I agree with E.V. Hill when he says, "Whatever God can get through you, He will get to you."

The book of Acts says, "It is more blessed to give than to receive." Giving is always the thermometer of our love for others. Eleanor Roosevelt said, "When you cease to make a contribution, you begin to die." If you have, give. If you lack, give.

Selfishness always ends in self-destruction. John Ruskin said, "When a man is wrapped up in himself, he makes a pretty small package." Henry Drummond said, "There is no happiness in having or in getting, but only in giving." The test of generosity is not necessarily how much you give but how much you have left. Henry Thoreau said, "If you give money, spend yourself with it." What you give, lives.

Does your reach exceed your grasp?

Stretching Exercises

Several years ago, I was awakened in the middle of the night with this thought, "Don't live within your means." Even though it was 4:30 a.m., I was so excited about this idea that I awoke my wife and began to "preach" to her about it for several minutes. (She said that the idea was great, but she really needed her sleep.)

What do I mean when I say, "Don't live within your means?" I believe we should act bigger, believe larger and associate higher. Your outlook determines your outcome. So, make your plans BIG.

I'm not encouraging you to go wild, to have no boundaries or be reckless. Certainly, we should spend within our means—but not live there. Talk with people smarter than you. Listen to those more spiritual than you. Ask questions of those more successful than you. Lend a hand to those less fortunate than you. Don't stay where you are.

If the shoe fits, don't wear it. You're not allowing room for growth. Webster knew all about the ineffectiveness of "living within your means." When you look up the word "means" in his dictionary, it tells you to see the word "average." When you decide to live within your means, you are deciding to live an average life. Do this: know your limits, then ignore them!

Do you put a question mark where God has put a period?

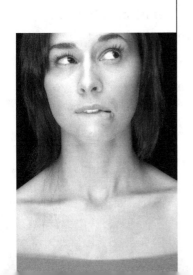

Proper Punctuation

"God never made a promise that was too good to be true," said D. L. Moody. "In everything you do, put God first, and He will direct you and crown your efforts with success" (Proverbs 3:6, TLB).

One of the great things about believing in God is found in Luke 18:27: "The things which are impossible with men are possible with God." When you join together with Him in His plan, things that were impossible now become possible. The superior man seeks success in God. The small man seeks success in himself or others.

You may trust the Lord too little, but you can never trust Him too much. With God's strength behind you, His love with you and His arms underneath you, together you can face the days ahead of you. "God is on our side," Abraham Lincoln wrote, "But it is more important to know that we are on God's side."

All great things have God involved in them. Dare to go with God farther than you can see. If something is beneficial for you, God will put it within your reach. "No good thing will He withhold from them that walk uprightly" (Psalm 84:11). A small man stands on others. A great man stands on God.

success in God

How much of you does God have?

Yield Signs

"If a man stands with his right foot on a hot stove and his left foot in a freezer, some statisticians would assert that, on the average, he is comfortable" *(Oral Hygiene)*. Nothing could be further from the truth. God doesn't want us to live our lives with one foot in heaven and one foot in the world. He wants all of us. There is something significant that happens when we become wholly yielded to Him.

"For the eyes of the Lord search back and forth across the whole earth, looking for people whose hearts are perfect toward Him, so that He can show His great power in helping them" (2 Chronicles 16:9, TLB).

D.L. Moody said: "It does not take long to tell where a man's treasure is. In fifteen minutes of conversation with most men, you can tell whether their treasures are on earth or in heaven."

As a young man, Billy Graham prayed, "God, let me do something—anything—for you." Look at the results of that simple prayer. When you have nothing left but God, then for the first time you become aware God is enough. The world has rarely seen what God can do with, for, and through a man who is completely yielded to Him. Martin Luther sums up being fully yielded this way: "God created the world out of nothing, and as long as we are nothing, He can make something out of us."

How old is your attitude?

Room for Self-Improvement

Have you ever noticed how many people you know who are literally at the same place today as they were five years ago? They still have the same dreams, the same problems, the same alibis, the same opportunities. They are standing still in life. It's as if people unplug their clocks at a certain point in time and stay at that fixed moment the rest of their lives.

You are destined to grow, learn and improve. Jesus said, "I have come that you might have life and life more abundantly." The biggest room in our lives is always the room for self-improvement.

I try to learn from everyone. From one I may learn what not to do, while from another, I learn what to do. Learn from the mistakes of others. You can never live long enough to make all the mistakes yourself. You can learn more from a wise man when he is wrong, than from a fool who is right.

The person who is afraid of asking is ashamed of learning. Only hungry minds can grow. It's true what W. Fussellman said, "Today a reader. Tomorrow a leader." It's fun to keep learning. Learning brings life to your life.

The last time someone asked, "What's new?" What was your answer?

Dream Fetchers

Get caught dreaming. It's never too late for you to start thinking more creatively. Often it is just a lack of imagination that keeps a person from his potential. Thinking of new ideas is like shaving: if you don't do it every day, you're a bum. Ask God to give you a flow of new, exciting and powerful ideas in your life.

Constantly frustrate tradition with your creativity and imagination. "Ideas are like rabbits. You get a couple and learn how to handle them, and pretty soon you have a dozen" (Anonymous). You'll get more out of every part of your life if you stay incurably curious.

"I'm a big fan of dreams. Unfortunately, dreams are the first casualty in life—people seem to give them up quicker than anything for a 'reality'" (Kevin Costner).

"The important thing is to not stop questioning. Never lose a holy curiosity" (Albert Einstein).

"Since it doesn't cost a dime to dream, you'll never short-change yourself when you stretch your imagination" (Robert Schuller).

I believe God left us in an unfinished world so we might share in the joys and satisfaction of creation. Creativity is built into every one of us; it's part of our design. Each of us lives less of the life intended for us when we choose not to use the creative powers we possess.

Will people say this about your life, "He did nothing in particular, and he did it very well?"

Life's Mission

Myles Monroe said, "There is something for you to start that is destined for you to finish." The purpose of life is to have a life of purpose.

John Foster said, "It is a poor disgraceful thing not to be able to reply, with some degree of certainty, to the simple questions, 'What will you be? What will you do?'" You're not truly free until you've been made captive by your mission in life.

A man without principle never draws much interest. William Cowper said, "The only true happiness comes from squandering ourselves for a purpose." Note Proverbs when it says, "Whatever your plan is, just know that nothing else will satisfy you."

The average person's life consists of 20 years of having parents ask where he or she is going, 40 years of having a spouse ask the same question and at the end, the mourners wondering the same thing. Martin Luther King, Jr. said, "If a man hasn't discovered something that he will die for, he isn't fit to live." You can predict your future by the awareness you have of your unique purpose. Abandon yourself to destiny.

Does the path you're on capture your heart?

Passion & Potential

One of the biggest differences in people is their level of
enthusiasm. Your enthusiasm reflects your reserves, your
unexploited resources and perhaps your future. You will
never rise to great heights without joy and enthusiasm.

"No one keeps up his enthusiasm automatically"
(Papyrus). Enthusiasm must be nourished with new
actions, new aspirations, new efforts and new vision. It's
your own fault if your enthusiasm is gone. You have failed
to feed it. What's enthusiasm? Henry Chester answers,
"Enthusiasm is nothing more or less than faith in action."
Helen Keller said, "Optimism is the faith that leads to
achievement." It simply means to be "full of God." Nothing
of real importance can be done without hope or confidence
in Him.

You can't deliver the goods if your heart is heavier
than the load. There is a direct correlation between our
passion and our potential. You could be the light of the
world, but no one will know it unless the switch is turned
on. Follow what the book of Ecclesiastes says, "Whatever
your hand finds to do, do it with all your might." I agree
with Winston Churchill when he said, "I am an optimist. It
does not seem too much use being anything else."

If revenge is sweet, why does it leave such a bitter taste?

Forgiveness Adventures

You can't get ahead while you're trying to get even.
Forgive your enemies—nothing annoys them more. There
is no revenge so sweet as forgiveness. The only people you
should try to get even with are those who have helped you.

Forgiveness ought to be like a cancelled note—torn in
two, and burned up, so that it never can be shown against
one" (Henry Ward Beecher). Never is God operating so
strong in your life as when you forego revenge and dare to
forgive an injury.

The one guaranteed formula for limiting your potential
is unforgiveness. Hate, bitterness and revenge are luxuries
none of us can afford. Forgive your enemies—you can't get
back at them any other way! Forgiveness saves the
expense of anger, the high cost of hatred and the waste of
energy.

If you want to be miserable, hate somebody.
Unforgiveness does a great deal more damage to the vessel
in which it is stored than the object on which it is poured.
To forgive is to set a prisoner free and discover the
prisoner was you" (Unknown).

Norman Cousins summed it up when he said, "Life is
an adventure in forgiveness."

Is fear causing you to run from something that isn't after you?

Butterfly Formation

Never trouble trouble until trouble troubles you. Arthur Roche said, "Worry is a thin stream of fear trickling through the mind. If encouraged, it cuts a channel into which all other thoughts are drained."

Sister Mary Tricky said, "Fear is faith that it won't work out." Instead, do what the book of 1 Peter says, "Let Him (God) have all your worries and cares, for He is always thinking about you and watching everything that concerns you."

Dr. Rob Gilbert advised, "It's all right to have butterflies in your stomach. Just get them to fly in formation." The great evangelist, Billy Sunday, once said, "Fear knocked at my door. Faith answered ... and there was no one there." Now that's the proper response to fear.

Fear can keep you from going where you could have won. Don't let your fears steal from you and prevent you from pursuing your dream. Most people believe their doubts and doubt their beliefs. So, do like the old saying and "feed your faith and watch your doubts starve to death." Worry is a route that leads from somewhere to nowhere; never let it direct your life.

What is one thing you can do for someone else who has no opportunity to repay you?

Serve High and Low

Serving others is one of life's most awesome privileges. Albert Schweitzer said, "The only ones among you who will really be happy are those who have sought and found how to serve." Hunt for the good points in people. Remember they have to do the same in your case. Then do something to help them. If you want to get ahead, be a bridge not a wall. Love others more than they deserve. Dr. Frank Crane said, "The golden rule is of no use unless you realize that it is your move." Each human being presents us with an opportunity to serve.

John Andrew Holmes said, "The entire population of the universe, with one trifling exception, is composed of others." Do you want to get along better with others? Be a little kinder than necessary. When you share, you do not lessen, but increase your life.

True leadership begins with servanthood. Harry Fosdick said, "One of the most amazing things ever said on earth is Jesus' statement, 'He that is greatest among you shall be your servant.' None have one chance in a billion of being thought of as really great a century after they're gone except those who have been servants of all."

Are you known by the promises you don't keep?

Lies Die Hard

Broken promises cause the world's greatest accidents. You can't make wrong work. Thomas Jefferson said, "Honesty is the first chapter of the book of wisdom." Never chase a lie: if you leave it alone, it will run itself to death. Everything you add to the truth, you inevitably subtract from it. It's discouraging to think how people nowadays are more shocked by honesty than by deceit.

"Those that think it is permissible to tell 'white lies' soon grow colorblind" (Awson O'Malley). We punish ourselves with every lie, and we reward ourselves with every right action. A lie will add to your troubles, subtract from your energy, multiply your difficulties and divide your effectiveness.

"Truth is always strong, no matter how weak it looks, and falsehood is always weak, no matter how strong it looks" (Marcus Antoninus). Never view anything positively that makes you break your word. Make your word your bond. The book of Proverbs says it best: "Dishonest gain will never last, so why take the risk?" Truth exists. Only lies are created. "If you continue to do what's right, what's wrong and who's wrong will eventually leave your life" (David Blunt).

Are you making dust or eating dust?

23

Dust Busters

When you run in place everyone will pass you by. Failure's most successful strategy is procrastination. *Now* is the best time to be alive and productive. If you want to make an easy job seem difficult, just keep putting off doing it. "We're all fugitives, and the things we didn't do yesterday are the bloodhounds" (Prism). Said Joseph Newton, "A duty dodged is like a debt unpaid; it is only deferred, and we must come back and settle the account at last."

What holds people back? "There are those of us who are always 'about' to live. We're waiting until things change, until there is more time, until we are less tired, until we get a promotion, until we settle down—until, until, until. It always seems that there is some major event that must occur in our lives before we begin living" (George Sheehan). *One* of these days is really *none* of these days.

"Do not allow idleness to deceive you; for while you give him today, he steals tomorrow from you" (H. Crowquill). Nothing is so fatiguing as the eternal hanging-on of an uncompleted task. "One day, today, is worth two tomorrows" (Ben Franklin).

What the fool does in the end, the wise person does in the beginning. Start, it's what will set you apart.

Be yourself. Who else is better qualified?

24

Take Full Account

Every person has specific gifts, talents and strengths. The book of Corinthians asserts, "Each man has his own gift from God." Incredibly, many actually spend their entire lives trying to change the way they were made. The Bible says when God made us it pleased Him (1 Corinthians 12:18). If God is pleased, shouldn't we be, too?

Marcus Aurelius said, "Take full account of the excellencies which you possess and in gratitude remember how you would hanker after them if you had them not." Too many people overvalue what they aren't and undervalue what they are. I agree with William Matthews when he said, "One well-cultivated talent, deepened and enlarged, is worth 100 shallow faculties."

Too many people take only their wants into consideration, never their talents and abilities. Deep down inside, if you are a musician, then make music. If you are a teacher, teach. Be what you are and you will be at peace with yourself. E.E. Cummings advised, "To be nobody but yourself—a world which is doing its best, night and day, to make you everybody else—means to fight the hardest battle which any human being can fight and never stop fighting." Abraham Lincoln said it best: "Whatever you are, be a good one."

What's the first small step you can take to get moving in the right direction?

25

Baby Steps

Small steps are a big idea. If you feel stuck, take small steps to get running again. Your future comes one hour at a time. Never be discouraged when you make progress, no matter how slow or small. Be only wary of standing still. Helen Keller said, "I long to accomplish a great and noble task but it is my chief duty to accomplish small tasks as if they were great and noble."

"Nobody makes the greater mistake than he who did nothing because he could only do a little" (Edmund Burke). One thing is certain: what isn't tried won't work. The most important thing is to begin, even though the first step is the hardest. I agree with Vince Lombardi: "Inches make champions." Take one small step right now. Don't ignore the small things. The kite flies because of its tail. It's the little things that count: sometimes a safety pin carries more responsibility than a bank president does.

Consider what Pat Robertson said: "Despise not the day of small beginnings because you can make all your mistakes anonymously." Value the little things. One day you may look back and realize they were the big things. Dante said, "From a little spark may burst a mighty flame." Remember this on your way up; the biggest dog was once a pup.

Do you count your blessings or think your blessings don't count?

26

Thank God for Dirty Dishes

To lose, you don't have to have anything stolen from you; all you have to do is take everything you have for granted. Today, replace regret with gratitude. Be grateful for what you have, not sorry for what you don't have. If you can't be thankful for what you have, then be thankful for what you have escaped. Joel Budd said: "I feel like I'm the one who wrote *Amazing Grace*." My two favorite words to God in prayer are, "Help!" and "Thanks!"

Capture what George Hubert said, "Thou O Lord hast given so much to me, give me one more thing—a grateful heart." It's a sure sign of mediocrity to be moderate with our thanks.

Don't find yourself at the end of your life saying, "What a wonderful life I've had! I only wish I'd appreciated and realized it sooner."

> Thank God for dirty dishes; they have a tale to tell.
> While other folks go hungry, we're eating pretty well.
> With home, and health, and happiness, we shouldn't want to fuss;
> For by this stack of evidence, God's been very good to us.

If you don't take action now, what will this ultimately cost you?

27

Tomorrow

If you wait too long, the future is gone before you get there. What you put off until tomorrow, you'll probably put off tomorrow, too. Success comes to the man who does today what others were thinking of doing tomorrow. The lazier a man is, the more he is going to do tomorrow.

> When duty comes a knocking at your gate,
> Welcome him in; for if you bid him wait,
> He will depart only to come once more
> And bring seven other duties to your door.
>
> (Anonymous)

In the game of life nothing is less important than the score at halftime. "The tragedy of life is not that man loses, but that he almost wins" (Haywood Broun). The things that come to a person who waits, seldom turn out to be the things they've waited for. Hard work is usually an accumulation of easy things that should have been done last week.

Jimmy Lyons said, "Tomorrow is the only day in the year that appeals to a lazy man." The book of Ecclesiastes says, "If you wait for perfect conditions, you'll never get anything done." The hardest work to do is that which should have been done yesterday.

Do your best friends bring out the best in you?

28

Losing Bad Company

Who you choose to be your closest friends or associates is one of the most important decisions you will make during the course of your life. "You are the same today that you are going to be in five years from now except for two things: the people with whom you associate and the books you read" (Charlie Jones). You do become like those you closely associate with.

A day away from the wrong associations is like a day in the country. The less you associate with some people, the more your life will improve. It's true what Proverbs says: "Putting confidence in an unreliable man is like chewing with a sore tooth, or trying to run on a broken foot."

Your true best friends are those who bring out the best in you. You are better, not worse, after you have been around them. Sometimes, a single conversation with the right person can be more valuable than many years of study.

The right kinds of friends are those with whom you can dare to be yourself, someone you can dream in front of aloud. For me, my best friends are those who understand my past, believe in my future and accept me today, just the way I am.

Who do you need to forgive?

29

Unpack for Peace

If you want to travel far and fast, then travel light. Unpack all of your envies, jealousies, unforgiveness, revenges, and fears. Be the first to forgive. Without forgiveness, life is governed by an endless cycle of resentment and retaliation. Think about it: is there anything as pathetic to behold as a person who has harbored a grudge and hatred for many years?

What really matters is what happens in us—not to us. "He who has not forgiven an enemy has never yet tasted one of the most sublime enjoyments of life," declares Johann Lavater. Forgiveness releases you and creates freedom.

One of the secrets of a long and fruitful life is to forgive everybody, everything, every night before you go to bed. Forgiving those who have wronged you is a key to personal peace. It is far better to forgive and forget than to hate and remember. Unforgiveness blocks blessings; forgiveness releases blessings.

Forgiveness won't change the past, but it will enlarge the future. Don't burn bridges. You'll be surprised how many times you have to cross over that same river. You'll "start your day on the right foot" if you ask yourself everyday, "Who do I need to forgive?"

What is one decision you would make if it would not fail?

30

The Risk Realm

It is amazing to me how many people decide in advance that they are going to fail and not reach their dreams. Those of us who believe in God can depend on what He said in the book of Philippians, "I can do everything God asks me to with the help of Christ who gives me the strength and power." God specializes in working beyond us.

Unless you enter the beehive, you can't take the honey. You and I are like rubber bands. We are most useful when we are stretched. Calvin Coolidge said, "We do not need more intellectual power, we need more spiritual power. We do not need more things that are seen, we need more of the things that are unseen." The reason so little is accomplished is generally because so little is attempted.

"It is not because things are difficult that we do not dare; it is because we do not dare that things are difficult" (Seneca).

The definition of impossible: something nobody can do until somebody does. Risk is part of every success plan. Bite off more than you can chew. "People who take risks are the people you'll lose against" (John Scully). You can't steal second base and keep your foot on first.

How many happy, selfish people do you know?

31

Avoiding Tunnel Vision

A man asked Dr. Carl Menninger, "What would you advise a person to do if he felt a nervous breakdown coming on?" Most people expected him to reply, "Consult a psychiatrist." To their astonishment he replied, "Lock up your house, go across the railroad tracks, find someone in need and do something to help that person."

"Nobody cares how much you know until they know how much you care" (John Cassis). Life is a lot like the game of tennis. Those who don't serve well, end up losing.

If you are dissatisfied with your lot in life, build a *service* station on it. A good way to forget your troubles is to help others out of theirs. Almost all of our unhappiness is the result of selfishness. Instead, think in terms of what the other person wants, not just what you want. It is absolutely true that you can succeed best and quickest by helping others succeed.

"The measure of life is not in its duration, but in its donation. Everyone can be great because everyone can serve" (Peter Marshall). No one achieves greatness without being of service. Never reach out your hand unless you're willing to extend an arm and your heart. Happiness is like potato salad—when shared with others, it's a picnic.

What are
you really
aiming at?

32

Stop Chasing Two Rabbits

You can do *more* by doing *less.* James Liter said, "One thought driven home is better than three left on base." Begin by delegating, simplifying, or eliminating low priorities as soon as possible. There are too many people in too many cars, in too much of a hurry, going too many directions, to get nowhere for nothing.

Follow this powerful advice from Paul the Apostle who wrote, "This *one* thing I do ... I press towards the mark." What you set your heart on, will determine how you will spend your life.

If you chase two rabbits, both will escape. Mark Twain said, "Behold the fool saith, 'Put not all thine eggs in one basket'—which is but a manner of saying, 'Scatter your money and your attention.' But the wise man saith, 'Put all your eggs in one basket—and watch that basket.'"

Vic Braden said, "Losers have tons of variety. Champions take pride in just learning to hit the same old boring winners." Consider what George Robson said after winning the Indianapolis 500: "All I had to do was keep turning left." We know that Walt Disney was successful. Maybe the key to his success is found in his confession: "I love Mickey Mouse more than any woman I've ever known." Now, that's focus!

What direction are your friends taking you?

33

Smooth Your Path with Noble Friends

Tell me who your best friends are, and I will tell you who you are. If you run with wolves, you will learn how to howl. But if you associate with eagles, you will learn how to soar to great heights. Proverbs says, "A mirror reflects a man's face, but what he is really like is shown by the kind of friends he chooses." The simple but true fact of life is that you become like those with whom you closely associate—for the good and the bad.

Think about it; almost all of our sorrows spring out of relationships with the wrong people. The *less* you associate with some people, the *more* your life will improve. Any time you tolerate mediocrity in others, it increases your mediocrity. I have found it is better to be alone, than in the wrong company.

If you find yourself taking two steps forward and one step backwards, invariably it's because you have mixed associations in your life. If a loafer isn't a nuisance to you, it's a sign that you are somewhat of a loafer yourself. Choose your associations carefully. This old saying is true: "He that lies down with dogs, shall rise up with fleas." Thomas Carlyle observed, "Show me the man you honor, and I will know what kind of man you are, for it shows me what your ideal of manhood is, what kind of man you long to be."

Are you becoming ordinary?

34

Imitation Is Limitation

When was the last time someone said to you "You're different!"? I believe that you and I are supposed to stand out, not blend in. Consider what 1 Peter 2:9 says, "But ye *are* a chosen generation, a royal priesthood, a holy nation, a peculiar people." Dare to be what you are. Think about it: Aren't most of the discontented people you know trying to be something they are not or trying to do something they're not supposed to do? Resolve to be yourself.

Most people live their entire lives as complete strangers to themselves. Don't let that happen to you. Leo Buscaglia counseled, "The easiest thing to be in the world is you. The most difficult thing to be is what other people want you to be. Don't let them put you in that position."

The opposite of courage is not fear. It's conformity. The most exhausting and frustrating thing in life is to live it trying to be someone else.

"My mother said to me, 'If you become a soldier you'll become a general, if you become a monk you'll end up as the pope.' Instead, I became a painter and wound up as Picasso," said the great artist. You can't become great by imitation. Imitation is limitation. Don't be a copy of something. Make your own impression.

Are you still growing, or just growing older?

35

Turning Points

Change. Does this word scare or inspire you? Herbert Spencer said, "A living thing is distinguished from a dead thing by the multiplicity of the changes at any moment taking place in it." Change is evidence of life. It is impossible to grow without change. The truth is, life is always at some turning point.

What people want is progress, if they can have it without change. Impossible! You must change and recognize that change is your greatest ally. The person who never changes his opinion, never corrects his mistakes. The fact is, the road to success is always under construction. Don't end up like concrete, all mixed up and permanently set. You cannot become what you are destined to be by remaining what you are. Do not fear change; it is the unchangeable law of increase. Don't be a person whose mind is always open to new ideas, provided they are the same old ones. Those who cannot change their minds cannot change anything. "There are people who not only strive to remain static themselves, but strive to keep everything else so ... their position is almost laughably hopeless" (Odell Shepard). All progress is due to those who were not satisfied to let well enough alone. They weren't afraid to change.

If you find an excuse, do you pick it up?

36

Drop It (The Excuse Habit)

When it comes to excuses, the world is full of great inventors. Failures are experts at making excuses. There are always enough excuses available if you are weak enough to use them.

Mistakes have hidden powers to help us, but they fail in their mission of helping us when we blame them on other people. When you use excuses, you give up your power to change and improve. "Never mind whom you praise, but be careful whom you blame" (Edmond Gosse). You can fall down many times, but you won't be a failure until you say that someone else pushed you.

So, find a way, not an excuse. Never complain and never explain. "Admitting errors clears the score and proves you wiser than before" (Arthur Guiterman). Doing a job right is always easier than fabricating an alibi for why you didn't. You waste time and creative energies thinking up excuses.

Nearly all failures come from people who have the habit of making excuses. The book of Proverbs says, "Work brings profit; talk brings poverty." If you're good at making excuses, it's hard to excel at anything else.

"If you don't have a dream, how are you going to make a dream come true?"

Oscar Hammerstein

37

Dream Engineering

Dare to think unthinkable thoughts. Develop an infinite capacity to ignore what others think can't be done. Life is too short to think small. Ronald McNair says, "You only become a winner if you are willing to walk over the edge." Take the lid off. Go out on a limb ... that's where the fruit is!

Most people could do more than they think they can, but they usually do less than they think they can. You never know what you cannot do until you try. I agree with Oscar Wilde when he said, "Moderation is a fatal thing. Nothing succeeds like excess." If you want to see if you can really swim, don't frustrate yourself with shallow water.

Dr. J.A. Holmes said, "Never tell a young person that something cannot be done. God may have been waiting for centuries for somebody ignorant enough of the impossible to do that thing. You will find that great leaders are rarely "realistic" by other people's standards.

Spirella writes:

There is no thrill in easy sailing when skies are clear and blue.

There is no joy in merely doing things which any man can do.

But there is some satisfaction that is mighty sweet to take,

When you reach a destination that you thought you would never make."

Are you a fanatic?

38

Risk Exposure

Have you ever met a highly successful person who wasn't "gung ho" about what he was doing with his life? Nothing significant was ever accomplished by a realistic person. For many years, "Safety first" has been the saying of the human race ... but it has never been the motto of leaders. A leader *must* face danger. He must take the risk, the blame and face the brunt of the storm" (Herbert Casson).

Dorthea Brand stated, "All that is necessary to break the spell of inertia and frustration is this: act as if it were impossible to fail." An over-cautious person burns bridges of opportunity before he gets to them. Most of the people who sit around and wait for the harvest haven't planted anything. The average person doesn't want much and usually gets even less.

Until you give yourself to some great cause, you haven't really begun to fully live. "Security is mostly a superstition. It does not exist in nature, nor do the children of men as a whole experience it. Avoiding danger is no safer in the long run than outright exposure. Life is either a daring adventure, or nothing" (Helen Keller).

What progress are you standing in the way of?

39

Pick the Right Person

"Our business in life is not to get ahead of others, but to get ahead of ourselves—to break our own records, to outstrip our yesterdays by today, to do our work with more force than ever before" (Stewart Johnson).

If you would like to know who is responsible for most of your troubles, take a look in the mirror. If you could kick the person responsible for most of your problems, you wouldn't be able to sit down for three weeks. It's time to stay out of our own way.

"Our best friends and our worst enemies are the thoughts we have about ourselves" (Dr. Frank Crane). Proverbs declares, "As a man thinks, so is he, and as a man chooses, so is he." Norman Vincent Peale remarked, "Do not build up obstacles in your imagination."

"Your future depends on many things, but mostly on you" (Frank Tyger). You may succeed if nobody else believes in you, but you will never succeed if you don't believe in yourself. Zig Ziglar observes, "What you picture in your mind, your mind will go to work to accomplish. When you change your pictures, you automatically change your performance." Whatever you attach consistently to the words, "I am," you will become.

Is your favorite letter "I"?

40

Self-Revolving Orbits

If we really stop to think about it, the cause of most of our problems is "I". "I want this ... I thought that ... I feel ... I ... I ... I." If you are only looking out for yourself, look out!

Wesley Huber said, "There is nothing quite so dead as a self-centered man—a man who holds himself up as a self-made success, and measures himself by himself and is pleased with the result." Don't become a legend in your own mind.

Norman Vincent Peale observed, "The man who lives for himself is a failure. Even if he gains much wealth, power or position, he is still a failure." Conceit makes us fools. The book of Proverbs reminds us, "Do you see a man wise in his own eyes? There is more hope for a fool than for him."

The man who believes in nothing but himself lives in a very small world. The best way to be happy is to forget yourself and focus on other people. The higher you go in life, the more dependent you become on other people. Work together with others. Remember the banana: every time it leaves the bunch, it gets peeled and eaten.

Forget yourself.

Work with others.

Are you a thermometer or a thermostat?

41

Be Your Own Gauge

Several years ago I met with a friend whom I have known for over ten years. He looked at me and said, "John, I see all the great things that are happening in your life and how you are increasing in so many different ways. But, as I began to look at *your* life, I became full of doubt as to what was happening in *my* life." He said, "It caused me to doubt myself because I had not had the same success that you have."

I turned, looked at him and said, "Well, if it's true that you feel bad because I've been successful, then would it be true that you would feel better if I had had terrible failures and had been doing much worse over the past several years?"

He gave me a quizzical look and responded, "No, that would not be true."

I replied, "Well, if it is true for one it is true for the other. Really, it shows how inaccurate your thinking is. What happens in my life has nothing to do with what is happening in your life."

A thermometer only responds to its outside environment for what direction to go. A thermostat determines its own temperature. Never measure your success by what others have or haven't done. It's never fair to compare.

When things go wrong, do you go with them?

42

Clean Up the Window

The time is always right to do the right thing. Be driven by excellence. The true measure of a person is in his height of ideals, the breadth of his sympathy, the depth of his convictions, and the length of his patience. Consider what the book of James says: "Therefore, to one who knows the right thing to do, and does not do it, to him it is sin."

If you want greatness, then forget greatness and earnestly pursue what is right. Then you can find both. Coach John Wooden said, "Success is peace of mind, which is a direct result of knowing you did your best to become the best that you are capable of being." Harold Taylor said, "The roots of true achievement lie in the will to become the best that you can become." Elevate your personal standards of quality. Whatever you thought was good enough for now, add 10 percent more. Stand for what's right, then you win, even if you "lose."

The biggest mistake you can make in life is not to be true to the best you know. George Bernard Shaw remarked, "Keep yourself clean and bright; you are the window through which you must see the world." Follow Ralph Sockman's advice: "Give the best that you have to the highest you know—and do it now."

Who's creating your world?

43

Your Decisions, Decisions

If you don't decide what's important in your life, someone else will decide for you. A wise person makes his own decisions; an ignorant one follows public opinion. Don't worry about not making a decision; someone else will make it for you, whether you like it or not.

Your destiny is not a matter of chance; it is a matter of choice. Get out of the middle of the road. Standing in the middle of the road is very dangerous; you can get knocked down by traffic coming from both directions.

A man with one watch knows what time it is; a man with two is never quite sure. Until you are decisively committed, there is hesitancy and the chance to draw back, followed by ineffectiveness. Listen to what you say. If you hear yourself saying, "I've decided," you're on the path towards an exciting and productive life. Decisions are what transform an idea into a reality.

A key to your future is that *you* can still choose, *you* can still decide. What you commit yourself to be will change you from what you are into what you can become. Decision determines destiny.

Is this a problem or a promotion?

44

The Breakfast of Champions

No obstacle will ever leave you the way it found you. You will either be better or worse. Problems are the price of progress. The obstacles of life are intended to make us better, not bitter. Adversity has advantages.

The truth is that if you like things easy, you will have difficulties. If you like problems, you will succeed. The biggest successes are the ones who solve the biggest problems. The Bible is a book of problems, filled with stories of men and women who faced incredible challenges, and with God's help overcame them and found themselves at another level.

The Chinese have a proverb that says, "The gem cannot be polished without friction, nor man perfected without trials." It seems that great trials are the necessary preparation for greatness. Consider what Jesus said: "Here on earth you will have many trials and sorrows; but cheer up, for I have overcome the world."

When you encounter obstacles, you will discover things about yourself that you never really knew. You will also find out what you really believe. Every problem introduces a person to himself. The breakfast of champions is not cereal; it's problems.

Do setbacks discourage or bring determination?

45

How to Finish First

Do you want to accomplish something in life? Be like the stone cutter. Jacob Riis says, "Look at the stone cutter hammering away at the rock, perhaps 100 times without as much as a crack showing in it. Yet at the 101st blow it will split in two, and I know it was not the last blow that did it, but all that had gone before." Whatever you want to accomplish in life will require persistence. Champion race car driver Rick Mears says, "To finish first you must first finish." Persistent people begin their success where most others quit.

Montesquieu said, "Success often depends on knowing how long it will take to succeed." The secret of success is: never let down and never let up. Consider what Proverbs says: "Seest thou a man diligent in his business? He shall stand before kings."

Ralph Waldo Emerson said, "The great majority of men are bundles of beginnings." Be like the bulldog: "The nose of the bulldog is slanted backwards so he can continue to breathe without letting go" (Winston Churchill).

Do you start your day in neutral?

46

Gearing up for Great Opportunity

How do you begin your day? Too many people lose an hour in the morning, and then spend the rest of the day trying to recapture it. Instead, start your day on the offensive. Be on the outlook for opportunities God is sending your way. Seize the moment! Opportunities are coming to you, or by you, every day. Today was once the future from which you expected so much in the past. Doing the best at this moment puts you in the best place for the next moment. When can you live if not now?

John Burroughs said, "The lesson which life repeats and constantly reinforces is, 'Look under foot.' You are always nearer than you think ... The great opportunity is where you are. Do not despise your own place and hour." The most important thing in our lives is what we are doing now. Know the real value of today.

The regrets that most people experience in life come from failing to act when having an opportunity. Albert Dunning said, "Great opportunities come to all, but many do not know that they have met them. The only preparation to take advantage of them is ... to watch what each day brings."

Are you backwards going forward?

47

Past Times

There is no future in the past. Mike Murdock said, "Stop looking at where you have been and start looking at where you can be." The past is always going to be the way it was. Stop trying to change it. Rosy thoughts about the future can't exist when your mind is full of the blues about the past.

The more you look back, the less you will get ahead. Thomas Jefferson was right when he said, "I like the dreams of the future better than the history of the past." I agree with Laura Palmer's advice: "Don't waste today regretting yesterday instead of making a memory for tomorrow." David McNally said, "Your past cannot be changed, but you can change your tomorrow by your actions today." Never let yesterday use up too much of today. The book of Proverbs says, "The wise man looks ahead. The fool attempts to fool himself and won't face the facts." It's true what Satchel Paige said: "Don't look back. Something may be gaining on you."

"Living in the past is a dull and lonely business; looking back strains the neck muscles, causing you to bump into people not going your way" (Edna Ferber). The first rule for happiness is: avoid lengthy thinking on the past. Nothing is as far away as one hour ago.

What benefit is running, if you're on the wrong road?

48

The Right Direction

Beverly Sills says, "There are no shortcuts to any place worth going." The way to the top is neither swift nor easy. Nothing worthwhile ever happens in a hurry—so be patient. Because of impatience, we are driven too soon from what we're supposed to do. Don't be impatient: remember, you can't warm your hands by burning your fingers.

Your success has less to do with speed and more to do with timing and direction. The key is doing the right thing at the right time. Lord Chesterfield said, "Whoever is in a hurry shows that the thing he is about is too big for him." There is simply more to life than increasing its speed. The trouble with life in the fast lane is that you get to the other end too soon. Haste makes waste; give time, time. Many people overestimate what they can do in a year and underestimate what they can do in a lifetime.

We are happiest when we discover that what we should be doing and what we are doing are the same things. I agree with what the book of Ecclesiastes says: "To everything there is a season, a time for every purpose under heaven." If you are facing the right direction, just keep on walking.

What would happen if you changed what you said about your biggest problem and your biggest opportunity?

49

Worthwhile Sayings

Recently I saw a sign under a mounted largemouth bass. It read: "If I had kept my mouth shut I wouldn't be here." How true! Don't jump into trouble, mouth first. What we say is important. Our daily commitment ought to be, "Oh, please fill my mouth with worthwhile stuff, and nudge me when I've said enough." Always speak less than you know.

A high school track coach was having difficulty motivating his team to perform at its best. The team developed the distinct reputation of coming in last at every track meet they entered. One factor contributing to his less than successful program was the coach's "pep talk" tactics. His most effective inspiring tool, he thought, was to tell his team, "Keep turning left and hurry back." Your words have the power to start fires or quench passion. The book of Job reminds us, "How forcible are right words."

If your lips would keep from slips;
Five things observe with care;
To whom you speak, of whom you speak,
And how, and when, and where.

"Are you motivated by what you really want out of life, or are you mass motivated?"

Earl Nightingale

50

True Security

"Every man must do two things alone," said Martin Luther. "He must do his own believing and his own dying." Making comparisons is a sure path to frustration. Comparison is never proof of anything. "You can't clear your own fields while counting the rocks on your neighbor's farm" Joan Welch). "The grass may be greener on the other side of the fence, but there's probably more of it to mow" (Lois Cory). Hills look small and green a long way off.

It's a waste of time and energy when you compare your life to that of other people. Life is more fun when you don't keep your score against others. Happiness can be found by doing what you do best and not worrying about what the other person is doing. Do you say, "I'm good, but not as good as I ought to be," or do you compare and say, "I'm not as bad as a lot of other people?" If I compare myself to John Grisham, I'll never write another book, but if I compare myself to Adolf Hitler, I'll think I'm a saint.

Don't think you're necessarily on the right road because it's a well-beaten path. The greatest risk in life is to wait for and depend on others for your security and satisfaction. The only standard to compare yourself to is God's Will and Word for your life.

Do you quit before you're finished?

51

Courage to Live

"The world will always give you the opportunity to quit, but only the world would call quitting an opportunity" (Clint Brown). One of the most powerful success principles ever preached is: **"Never, never, never give up!"** (Winston Churchill)

A lazy man is always judged by what he doesn't do. The choice of giving up or going on is a defining moment in your life. Nobody and nothing can keep you down unless you decide not to rise again. H.E. Jansen said, "The man who wins may have been counted out several times, but he didn't hear the referee." Find a way to, not a way *not* to.

Too many people stop faster than they start. Instead of stopping, follow this English proverb: "Don't fall before you are pushed." Margaret Thatcher understood the principle of not quitting when she advised, "You may have to fight a battle more than once to win it." David Zucker added, "Quit now, you'll never make it. If you disregard this advice you'll be halfway there."

The choice is simple. You can either stand up and be counted, or lie down and be counted out. Your success will be measured by your willingness to keep on trying. Have the courage to live. Anyone can quit.

Are you content with failure?

52

Take on Wings

Have you ever failed or made a mistake? The fact that you've failed is proof that you're not finished. Failures and mistakes can be a bridge, not a barricade, to success. Because, it's not how far you fall, but how high you bounce that makes all the difference.

One of the riskiest things you can do in life is to take too many precautions and never have any failures or mistakes. No one has ever achieved genuine success who did not, at one time or another, teeter on the edge of disaster. If you have tried to do something and failed, you are vastly better off than if you had tried to do nothing and succeeded. If you're not making mistakes, you're not risking enough.

Success consists of getting up just one time more than you fall down. So, get up and go on. Proverbs says, "A man who refuses to admit his mistakes can never be successful, but if he confesses and forsakes them, he gets another chance."

Failure can become a weight or it can give you wings. The only way to make a comeback is to go on, and ninety-- nine percent of success is built on former failure. The truth is we're like a tea bag: not worth much until we've been through some hot water.

Which would you rather have: a bouquet of flowers or a packet of seeds? Laurie Beth Jones

53

Keep Planting

An overnight success? Get rich quick? Instant gratification? We live in an instant era; we want it now. We don't really want to take the "seeds." We want the flowers. The truth is, the path of persistence pays.

Never give up on what you really know you should do. Failure is waiting on the path of least persistence. The "man of the hour" spent many days and nights getting there. Consider the man who said, "My overnight success was the longest night of my life." The truth is, an overnight success takes about ten years. Most people don't realize how close they are to success when they quit. Remember, stopping at third base adds no more score than striking out.

When you're persistent, it's proof you have not been defeated. Mike Murdock says, "You have no right to anything you have not pursued. For the proof of desire is in the pursuit." Life holds no greater wealth than that of steadfast commitment. It cannot be robbed from you. Only you can lose it by your will.

The secret of success is to start from scratch and keep on scratching. We evaluate people by what they finish, not by what they start. People do not fail; they just quit too soon.

persistence

Are you deliberately planning on being less than you are capable of being?

HARD HAT
AREA

54

A Work In Progress

"Eli Whitney was laughed at when he showed his cotton gin. Edison had to install his electric light free of charge in an office building before anyone would even look at it. The first sewing machine was smashed to pieces by a Boston mob. People scoffed at the idea of railroads. People thought that traveling thirty miles an hour would stop the circulation of the blood. Morse had to plead before ten Congresses before they would even look at his telegraph" (Anonymous). Yet for all these men, the sky was not the limit.

"Beware of those who stand aloof and greet each venture with reproof; the world would stop if things were run by men who say, 'It can't be done'" (Samuel Glover).

We achieve in proportion to what we attempt. More people are persuaded into believing in nothing than into believing too much. "Where there is no vision the people perish," says the book of Proverbs. You can start today and with God's help, begin to move forward. Here's good news: God isn't finished with you yet.

the sky is NOT the limit

move forward

What's the best use of your time right now?

55

Live in the Present

Right now is the most important time. The reason most people don't go very far in life is because they sidestep opportunity and shake hands with procrastination. Procrastination is the grave in which opportunity is buried. For the tenacious, there is always time and opportunity. Don't sit back and take what comes, go after what you want. Albert Hubert remarked, "Parties who want milk should not seat themselves on a stool in the middle of the field and hope that the cow will back up to them." The door of opportunity won't open unless you push.

I agree with Jonathan Winters: "I couldn't wait for success—so I went ahead without it." "A wise man will make more opportunities than he finds," said Francis Bacon.

Life is full of golden opportunities. Every person has a lot that he or she can do. Start with what you can do; don't stop because of what you can't do. Great opportunities will come as you make the most of small ones. Many people seem to think that opportunity means a chance to get money without earning it. The best gifts we get are opportunities, not things. Seize them!

Do you still believe that anything is possible, or have you come to know better?

56

Visioning

The person with imagination is never alone and never finished. You were created for creativity. Your eyes are designed to look for opportunity and your ears to listen for direction. Your mind requires a challenge and your heart longs for the best way.

Make a daily demand on your creativity. Everything great started as somebody's daydream. Successful people are first dreamers. "We are told never to cross a bridge until we come to it, but this world is owned by men who have 'crossed bridges' in their imagination far ahead of the crowd" (Speakers Library).

Grandmother saw Billy running around the house slapping himself and asked him why. "Well," said Billy, "I just got so tired of walking that I thought I'd ride my horse for a while."

One day Michelangelo saw a block of marble that the owner said was of no value. "It is valuable to me," said Michelangelo. "There is an angel imprisoned in it, and I must set it free." Learn to see the unseen.

Is God finished with you yet?

57

Strength Training

The late astronaut James Irwin said, "You might think going to the moon was the most scientific project ever, but they literally 'threw us' in the direction of the moon. We adjusted our course every ten minutes and landed inside fifty feet of the 500 mile radius of our target." On that mission, every change, no matter how small, was essential to success. God does that for us. Psalm 138:8 says: "The Lord will perfect that which concerns me."

Everyone wants to change the world, but no one thinks of changing himself. "Poverty and shame shall be to him that refuses instruction: but he that regards reproof shall be honored" (Proverbs). Unwillingness to accept your present creates a future. "Better to be pruned to grow than cut up to burn," said John Trapp. A bad habit never goes away by itself. "It's always an undo-it-yourself project" (Abigail Van Buren).

Wise people sometimes change their minds—fools never do. Be open to changes in your plans. It is a sign of strength to make changes when necessary.

The road to success is always under construction. Success and growth are unlikely if you always do things the way you've always done them.

open to change

Both enthusiasm and pessimism are contagious. How much of each do you spread?

58

Words Have Power

Your words reflect what you believe about your future. Just to see how it feels, for the next twenty-four hours refrain from saying anything bad about anyone or anything. "The difference between the right word and almost the right word is the difference between lightning and the lightning bug," said Mark Twain.

The person who finds the negative seldom finds anything else. Live your life as an exclamation, not an explanation. Children are born optimists; then the world slowly tries to educate them out of their "delusion." The fact is, the more you complain the less you'll obtain.

Some people always find the bad in a situation. Do you know people like that? Think about it; how many successful complainers do you know? Many a great idea has been quenched by wrong words. Don't spend your life standing at the complaint counter.

A wise old owl sat on an oak,
The more he saw the less he spoke;
The less he spoke the more he heard;
Why aren't we like that wise old bird?

(Edward H. Richards)

Are you a person who says, "Ready, aim, aim, aim?"

59

Focus Improves Your Aim

Opportunity is all around you. What matters is where you put your focus. Ask yourself this question every day: "Where should my focus be?" Where you focus your attention, you create strength and momentum.

Concentration is the key that opens the door to accomplishment. "The first law of success ... is concentration—to bend all the energies to one point, and to go directly to that point, looking neither to the right nor to the left" (William Mathews).

I am astonished at the aimlessness of most people's lives. There is a great distance between most peoples' dreams and the results they achieve. As a result of a lack of focus, they delegate the direction of their lives to others. Don't live your life like that.

We can accomplish things by directing our desires, not by ignoring them. What an immense power you will have over your life when you possess distinct aims. Your words, the tone of your voice, your dress, your very motions change and improve when you begin to live for a definite reason.

Don't be a person who is uncertain about the future and hazy about the present. Make something your specialty. To finish the race, stay on the track.

If you don't enjoy what you have, how could you be happier with more?

60

A Bounty of Blessings

Think thanks. Be aggressively thankful. No duty is more urgent than that of returning thanks. The person who isn't thankful for what he's got, isn't likely to be thankful for what he's going to get. Ingratitude never ends.

Thanksgiving, you will find, creates power in your life because it opens the generators of your heart to respond gratefully, to receive joyfully and to react creatively. William Ward spoke wisely: "There are three enemies of personal peace: regret over yesterday's mistakes, anxiety over tomorrow's problems and ingratitude for today's blessing."

We all have a lot to be thankful for. For example: No matter what house you live in, wouldn't you rather be there than the best hospital in your city? If you can't be satisfied with what you've reached, be thankful for what you've escaped. The words *think* and *thank* come from the same Latin root. If we take time to *think* more, we will certainly *thank* more. I like what Dwight L. Moody said: "Be humble or you'll stumble."

The most highly satisfied life can be found in being thankful. Appreciative words are one of the most powerful forces for good on the earth. Thankful words don't cost much, yet they accomplish so much. So, count your blessings; don't discount them.

Are you being criticized?

61

Frontrunning

People who are growing with God all share one common trait; they attract criticism. Criticism is a compliment when you are doing what you know you're supposed to do.

I was reading a cover story on Billy Graham in *Time* magazine a couple of years ago and was surprised to find in that article several criticisms of him from fellow ministers. Then I was reminded of this fact: all great people get great criticism. Learn to accept and expect that you will receive unjust criticisms for your God-given goals and accomplishments.

It can be beneficial to receive constructive criticism from those who have your best interests at heart, but you're not responsible to respond to those who don't. I like what Edward Gibbon said: "I never make the mistake of arguing with people for whose opinions I have no respect."

It's a thousand times easier to criticize than create. That's why critics are never problem solvers. My feeling is that the person who says it cannot be done, should not interrupt the one who is doing it. Don't waste time responding to your critics, because you owe nothing to a critic. Just remember, when you are kicked from behind, it means you are out in front.

Is it a long way from your words to your deeds?

62

The Action Attraction

"People judge you by your actions, not your intentions. You may have a heart of gold, but so does a hard boiled egg" (*Good Reading*). A thousand words will not leave as lasting an impression as one deed.

Some people spend their whole time searching for what's right, but then they can't seem to find any time to practice it. Your life story is not written with a pen, but with your actions.

Momentum doesn't just happen. "The common conception is that motivation leads to action, but the reverse is true—action precedes motivation" (Robert McKain). "Shun idleness. It is a rust that attaches itself to the most brilliant of metals" (Voltaire). Ironically, idleness is persistent. It keeps on and on, but soon enough it arrives at poverty.

Henry Ford once commented, "You can't build a reputation on what you're going to do." A man of words and not of deeds is like a flowerbed full of weeds. Don't let weeds grow around your dreams. To only dream of the person you would like to be is to waste the person you are. Don't just dream of great accomplishments; stay awake and do them.

What
works?

63

Check out the Ceiling

What you *can* do—you can *do*. Whatever works, work on that. Don't wish you could do things you can't do. Instead focus and build on what is already working.

Everyone who got where he is, had to begin where he was. Only a few people really know how to live in the present. The problem is that we seldom think of what we have; instead, we think of what we lack.

"We don't need more strength or more ability or greater opportunity. What we need to use is what we have" (Basil Walsh). People are always ignoring something they can do while trying to do something they can't. Learning new things won't help the person who isn't using what he already knows. Success means doing the best we can with what we have.

Norman Vincent Peale said, "We've all heard that we have to learn from our mistakes, but I think it is more important to learn from our successes. If you learn only from your mistakes, you are inclined to learn only errors." "Every ceiling, when reached, becomes a floor upon which one walks and now can see a new ceiling. Every exit is an entry somewhere" (Tom Stoppard).

Do you tackle problems bigger than you?

64

Big Dipper

People nearly always pick a problem their own size and ignore or leave to others the bigger or smaller ones. Pick a problem that's bigger than you. "Success, real success, in any endeavor demands more from an individual than most people are willing to offer—not more than they are capable of offering" (James Roche).

"One who is contented with what he has done will never be famous for what he will do" (Christian Bovee). If you have achieved all you have planned for yourself, you have not planned enough. Be used for something significant. Choose a goal for which you are willing to exchange a piece of your life. The surest way to happiness is to lose yourself in a cause greater than yourself. If God is your partner, make your plans BIG.

To be completely satisfied with yourself is a sure sign that progress is about to end. To small thinkers, everything looks like a mountain. "It is difficult to say what is impossible, for the dream of yesterday is the hope of today and the reality of tomorrow" (Robert Goddard). The grandest things are, in some ways, the easiest to do because there is so little competition.

God is your partner

Are you ready?

65

Expect to Receive

To one person the world is desolate, dull and empty; to another the same world looks rich, interesting and full of meaning. "Eyes that look are common. Eyes that see are rare," says J. Oswald Sanders. If you look at life the wrong way, there is always cause for alarm. It's the same way a twenty-dollar bill can look so big when it goes to church and so small when it goes for groceries. What you see depends mainly on what you look for.

Position yourself to receive, not resist. "Any fact facing us is not as important as our attitude toward it, for that determines our success or failure" (Norman Vincent Peale). When you are positioned right, opportunity presents itself. Opportunity can be missed if you are broadcasting when you should be tuning in. Opportunities can drop in your lap, if you have your lap where opportunities drop.

Most people have trouble with the future because it arrives before they are ready for it. You'll find that life responds to your outlook. We go where our vision is. Life is mostly a matter of expectation. "For I know the plans I have for you, declares the Lord. Plans to prosper you and not to harm you, plans to give you a hope and a future" (Jeremiah 29:11).

Who gives you more trouble than you?

Solve the Problem

Here's the first rule of winning: don't beat yourself. Have you found that your biggest enemy is you? Dwight L. Moody said it best when he said, "I have never met a man who has given me as much trouble as myself."

Most of the important battles we face will be waged within ourselves. There are two forces warring against each other inside us. One says, "You can't!" The other says, "You can!" Be encouraged by this fact found in the book of Matthew, "With God all things are possible."

The basic problem most people have is that they are doing nothing to solve their basic problem. This problem is: they build a case against themselves. They are their own worst enemy. Don't put water in your own boat, the storms of life will put enough in on their own.

We lie loudest when we lie to ourselves. "You can't consistently perform in a manner that is inconsistent with the way you see yourself," says Zig Ziglar. Determine to multiply your commitment, divide your distractions, subtract your excuses and add your faith. The first key victory you must win is over yourself.

Do you quit after a victory?

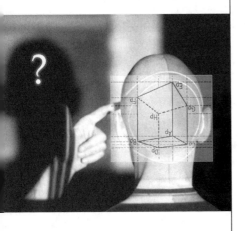

67

Develop New Plans

There are two times when a person is likely to quit, after a failure or after a victory. Instead, if at first you do succeed, try something harder. All progress is due to those who were not satisfied to let well enough alone. "Acorns were good until bread was found," said Sir Francis Bacon. The majority of men fail because of their lack of persistence in creating new plans to improve those that succeed.

Do more than is required and continue doing it. "The difference between ordinary and extraordinary is that little extra," says Zig Ziglar. There is always a way—then there is always a better way. When you've found something— look again. "It's what you learn after you know it all that counts," says John Wooden. A successful man continues to look for work after he has found a job.

"Show me a thoroughly satisfied man, and I will show you a failure," said Thomas Edison. "There are two kinds of men who never amount to very much," Cyrus H.K. Curtis remarked to his associate, Edward Bok. "And what kinds are those?" inquired Bok. "Those who cannot do what they are told," replied the famous publisher, "and those who can do nothing else." Find a better way, and make that way better.

How many people of great potential have you known?

Where did they all go?

68

Forward Motion

Potential can be one of the emptiest words in the world. Potential is important, but what you do with your God-given talent is much more important. A person has a success or two and is labeled with "potential greatness." Then the biggest trap presents itself: quitting after a victory. Success has made failures of many people.

Once you're moving, you can keep moving. Did Michael Jordan stop shooting after making his first basket? Did Max Lucado quit writing after his first best seller? Successful people know that each victory buys an admission ticket to a more challenging opportunity. The more you do, the more you can do.

"Perhaps it is a good thing that you haven't seen all your dreams come true. For when you get all you wish for, you will be miserable. To be forever reaching out, to remain unsatisfied is a key to momentum" (*North Carolina Christian Advocate*).

Stop and smell the roses along the journey, just don't stay so long that the petals have dropped, the limbs have been pruned and all that's left is the thorns. It's not what you get that makes you successful; rather, it is what you are continuing to do with what you've got that's a better yardstick.

Do you give up control of your life to something other than faith?

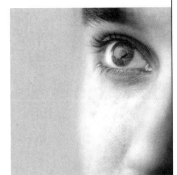

69

Faith-lifts

Everyone needs a "faith-lift." "The only thing that stands between a man and what he wants from life is often merely the will to try it and the faith to believe that it is possible" (Richard DeVos). Faith can rewrite your future. God always holds something for the man who keeps his faith in Him. " ... He is a rewarder of them that diligently seek Him" (Hebrews 11:6). Your life will shrink or expand in proportion to your faith.

A.W. Tozer wrote: "Real faith is not the stuff dreams are made of; rather it is tough, practical, and altogether realistic. Faith sees the invisible but it does not see the non-existent." Corrie ten Boom described faith this way: "It is like radar that pierces through the fog, the reality of things at a distance that the human eye cannot see."

The world says that seeing is believing. Faith says that believing is seeing. Faith is like a toothbrush. You should have one and use it daily, but you shouldn't try to use someone else's. Doubt is the great modern plague, but faith can cure it.

Doubt sees the obstacle, faith sees the way;
Doubt sees the darkest night, faith sees the day;
Doubt dreads to take a step, faith soars on high;
Doubt questions, "Who believes?"
Faith answers, "I."

(Anonymous)

If everyone in the United States were on your level of spirituality, would there be revival in the land?

70

Service Checklist

What kind of world would this be if everyone was just like you? Change begins with you. Remember when you are pointing your finger at someone else, there are three pointing back at you. When confronted with a new opportunity or tough situation, I usually ask myself, "Do I have a pure heart and a right spirit?" Psalm 139: 23-24 prays, "Search me, O God, and know my heart; try me, and know my thoughts; and see if there be any wicked way in me, and lead me in the way everlasting."

James Allen said, "You will become as small as your controlling desire; as great as your dominant aspiration." If a person's aim in this world is right, he will miss *fire* in the next. Roger Babson added, "If things are not going well with you, begin your effort at correcting the situation by carefully examining the service you are rendering and especially the spirit in which you are rendering it."

To know what is right and not do it is as bad as doing wrong. Nothing costs more than doing the wrong thing. The man who borrows trouble is always in debt. The best way to escape evil is to pursue good. Pastor Joel Budd said, "A hungry heart is like a parachute. When you pull on it, it opens up and saves you." Keep your head and heart going in the right direction and you won't have to worry about your feet.

Change begins with you.

My Questions Have Answers

- God's my heavenly Father and I'm His child.
- He will never leave me or forsake me.
- He calls me a friend.
- He holds the keys to death and life.
- Nothing can separate me from the love of God.
- I can trust Him.
- He has known me since the beginning of time and has written my name in the palm of His hand.
- He forgives me when I ask Him to.
- He's concerned about what concerns me.
- God has all power in heaven and earth.
- He gives His angels charge over me.
- He is able to do exceedingly, abundantly, above all that I can ask or think.
- He wants me to prosper and be in health, even as my soul prospers.
- He's with me in this room right now.
- He knows every thought I have, sees everything I do and hears everything I say.
- There is a heaven and I am going there.

About the Author

John Mason is a minister, best-selling author, and international speaker. He is founder and president of Insight International, an organization dedicated to helping people use all their gifts and talents while fulfilling God's plan for their lives.

Mason has authored many books including *An Enemy Called Average*, *You're Born an Original—Don't Die a Copy*, *Let Go of Whatever Makes You Stop*, and *Conquering an Enemy Called Average*, which have sold over 1.3 million copies. His latest books are *Know Your Limits—Then Ignore Them*, and a devotional prayer book, *Proverbs Prayers*.

His books are known as a source of godly wisdom, scriptural motivation, and practical principles. They have been translated into twenty-six languages around the world. John lives in Tulsa, Oklahoma with his wife, Linda, and their four children.

You may contact John for speaking or prayer requests at:

Insight International

8801 South Yale Avenue, Suite 410

Tulsa, OK 74137

Phone: (918) 493-1718

E-mail: contact@freshword.com

Website: www.freshword.com